A 3-minute forever book

EAT
YOUR
PEAS

for Gardening Friends

By Cheryl Karpen
Gently Spoken Communications

Dedicated to my sister,
Darlene,
who introduced me
to the

joy of digging

Transplanted
from
my heart to yours.

To
Little Debbi

with love from

" By al "

More than anything, I must have flowers, always, always.

Claude Monet

This little book
is
blooming
with a promise.
It's
a
promise
from me to you
and
it goes like this:

The next time you feel like there's
a hundred-pound sack of soil on your back
or the weeds upon your path have a chokehold on life,
Call me.

I promise to listen. Really listen.
We'll talk if you want. Cry if we need to.
Even find something to make us laugh.
In other words, I promise to be there for you.

Just call me.

In the meantime,
here's a little **homegrown wisdom**
from one **gardening friend** to another.

May it brighten your day
and lighten your load.

Indispensable tools for *gardening*:

Shovel
Gloves
Hoe
Clippers
and a
watering can

Indispensable tools for *life*:

Grace
Gratitude
Faith
Love
and
You!

The hardiest climbers in the world still need sturdy support to show their stuff.

Why should friends be any different?

I'll be your trellis if you'll be mine!

Don't even think about
weeding your garden
before I come over!

I love you just the way you are.

Abundance
Beauty
Fortitude
RE-creation
Patience
Transformation

A garden is a masterful teacher.

The potting shed:
a place where you can
get caught up on the latest dirt,
spill a few beans,
and never break a confidence.

Compost happens.

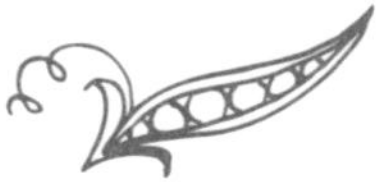

Ahh Springtime...

Time to breathe deeply,
plan carefully, review your budget,
then **go to your favorite nursery**
and get completely carried away!

·COUPON·
A trip to the
Greenhouse
...together!

Topsoil for the soul...

Pansies represent loving thoughts

Cornflowers are for healing

Thyme gives us strength and courage

Violets represent faithfulness

Johnny Jump-ups are full of happy thoughts

Lily of the Valley are filled with a return to happiness

Plant seeds of optimism
and see how they
pollinate everything
(and everyone !)
that comes near them.

Lush growth and vibrant color are seldom possible without **courageous pruning**.

Good friends are like sun showers.
Full of surprises.
Brimming with light.

Reasons why your mother told you to
eat your peas:

1. They really are **good for you**—
   vitamins, iron, and all that.

2. There's no better **finger food**
   right out of the garden.

3. They're **good practice**—
   if you can eat peas with a fork,
   you can eat anything!

Go
forth
and
multiply.

Color your garden with sweet abandon!

Color	Emotion	Flower
Red	Passion	Daylilies, Zinnias
Yellow	Hope and Optimism	Daffodil, Yarrow
Lavender	Divinity	Bellflowers, Crocus
Orange	Playful	Chinese Lantern, Marigolds
Green	Harmony	Lady's Mantel
Pink	Upbeat	Sweet Pea, Foxglove
Blue	Tranquility	Columbine, Hyacinth
White	Peace	Phlox, Hydrangea

When you plant bulbs
in the fall,
do it for all you're worth!

There's no greater way to declare
your **faith in the future**
of all things
bright and beautiful.

Let's have
a

plant swapping party.

We'll invite all of our garden loving friends,
share coveted cuttings,
and down-to-earth advice.

Rule of the Order of Green Thumbs

I. No matter what, time will be taken to **sit in the garden every morning** as close to the first light as one's internal clock allows. **Bare feet** recommended.

II. Particular attention will be paid to the following sensations:

Sunshine on the face.

Scent in the air? Early songbird.

And dew underfoot.

Caution: May induce euphoria. Reported side effects include drowsiness, nostalgia and the inability to move.

How to develop a strong root system:

1. Water well.
2. Provide good nourishment.
3. Be ruthless with weeds.
4. Celebrate sunshine wherever you find it.

Some
say a garden
is a
gift from God.

I say that goes for friendships too—
which means **a friend like you**
in my garden
must surely be **heaven on earth!**

A
garden
is a place where
grown ups get to play
in the dirt.

Mudpies anyone?

If perennials can survive
winter freezes
and
outrageous weather...

so can we!

Gifts of the garden

A hide-away
for the heart

An invitation
to quiet

A tease of color

A serenade
for the soul

A sanctuary for
family and friends

An excuse to get
good and dirty

Cultivate a
garden

rich in friendship and family.

During times of drought,
they will sustain you with love
and keep you grounded
through rocky times.

Some of the people we meet
are like annuals — lovely enough,
but they only stay for awhile.

Other **people** in our lives
are more like **perennials** —
they come back to us
again and again,
growing more beautiful
with each passing year.
Thank you for being
an heirloom perennial
in my garden.

In the true spirit of gardening,

 plant abundantly,

sow seeds of goodness,

sprout love, hope, and compassion,

wherever you go

and most of all stay healthy.

Remember to always...

(plant)
eat your peas!

Love you always
Mia. ♡ B B

Why Peas?

She was a vibrant, dazzling young woman with a promising future.
Yet, at sixteen, her world felt sad and hopeless.

I was living over 1800 miles away and wanted to let this very special young person in my life know I would be there for her across the miles and through the darkness. I wanted her to know she could call me any time, at any hour, and I would be there for her. And I wanted to give her a piece of my heart she could take with her anywhere—a reminder she was loved.
Really loved.

Her name is Maddy and she was the inspiration for my first PEAS book, **Eat Your Peas for Young Adults**. At the very beginning of her book I made a place to write in my phone number so she knew I was serious about being available. And right beside the phone number I put my promise to listen—really listen—whenever that call came.

Soon after the book was published, people began to ask me if I had the same promise and affirmation for adults. I realized it isn't just young people who need to be reminded how truly special they are. We all do.

Today Maddy is thriving and giving hope to others in her life.
If someone has given you this book it means you are a pretty amazing person to them and they wanted to let you know. Take it to heart.

Believe it, and remind yourself often.

Wishing you peas and plenty of joy,

Cheryl Karpen

P.S. If you are wondering why I named the collection, Eat Your Peas...it's my way of saying, "Stay healthy. I love and cherish you. I want you to live **forever**!"

My garden GROWS with GRATITUDE for...

Amazing Artist, Sandy Fougner

Sandy, your artistry turned this book into a secret garden
blooming with creativity and imagination.
Thank you for so passionately sharing your gift
with the rest of us gardening folk.

Editor with heart, Suzanne Foust

You are a true artist of words. What a treasure to behold!

A special thank you to: Gina Little, Linda Atherton,
Deborah Cowan, Lana Siewert-Olson and to all the
other individuals who continue to believe in me.
You are a blessing in my life.

Cheryl
2004

Other books by Cheryl Karpen

The Eat Your Peas™ Collection

Takes only 3-minutes to read but you'll want to hold on to it forever!

Eat Your Peas™ for Daughters
Eat Your Peas™ for Sisters
Eat Your Peas™ for Girlfriends
Eat Your Peas™ for Mothers
Eat Your Peas™ for Young Adults

New titles are SPROUTING up all the time!

Hope and Encouragement Collection

To Let You Know I Care
Hope for a Hurting Heart
Can We Try Again? Finding a way to love

Eat Your Peas™ for Gardening Friends

Copyright 2002, Cheryl Karpen

For more information or to locate a store near you contact:

Gently Spoken Communications
P.O. Box 245
Anoka, Minnesota 55303
1-877-224-7886
www.gentlyspoken.com